BOSNIA-HERZEGOVINA
in Pictures

Mary Englar

Twenty-First Century Books

Contents

Website address: www.lernerbooks.com

Twenty-First Century Books
A division of Lerner Publishing Group
241 First Avenue North
Minneapolis, MN 55401 U.S.A.

web enhanced @ www.vgsbooks.com

Library of Congress Cataloging-in-Publication Data

Englar, Mary.
    Bosnia-Herzegovina in pictures / by Mary Englar.
      p. cm. — (Visual geography series)
    Includes bibliographical references and index.
    ISBN-13: 978-0-8225-2393-2 (lib. bdg. : alk. paper)
    ISBN-10: 0-8225-2393-0 (lib. bdg. : alk. paper)
    1. Bosnia and Hercegovina—Pictorial works— 1. Juvenile literature. 2. Bosnia and Hercegovina—Juvenile literature. I. Title. II. Series: Visual geography series (Minneapolis, Minn.)
    DR1662.E54 2007
    949.74203'022'2—dc22
                                          2005004652

Manufactured in the United States of America
1 2 3 4 5 6 – BP – 12 11 10 09 08 07

INTRODUCTION

With thousands of global peacekeeping troops on its soil, Bosnia-Herzegovina (often called just Bosnia) is maintaining a fragile peace after the brutal civil war of the 1990s, which tore apart the region. Bosnia-Herzegovina was once part of Yugoslavia, ruled for thirty-five years by Communist dictator Josip Broz (Tito). Yugoslavia included six diverse republics, all united by the strength of Tito, who suppressed ethnic differences and held the nation together.

But when Tito died in 1980 and Communist governments collapsed around the world in the early 1990s, everything changed. Old ethnic differences resurfaced. Across Yugoslavia, people of different ethnic groups and geographical regions started to think about independence. Without Tito to hold them together, the six republics were no longer united. Civil war soon followed. The Yugoslavian government, dominated by Serbia (one of the six republics), struggled to hold the nation together in the regions of Slovenia, Croatia, and Bosnia. But many of the people in these republics didn't feel represented in the Yugoslavian

government and were determined to have independence.

The violence and hatred of the conflicts that followed shocked the world. The worst of the violence came in Bosnia, where ethnic Serbs, Bosniaks (Bosnian Muslims), and ethnic Croats battled for power. News reports exposed "ethnic cleansing" and mass graves. Photos showed gaunt war prisoners behind barbed wire fences. Reporters told of people in the city of Sarajevo fleeing to avoid the fire of snipers hidden in the hills above the city. Entire villages had been burned to the ground.

Out of this terrible fighting emerged several new nations, including Bosnia-Herzegovina. But Bosnia-Herzegovina is more than the war images suggest. For more than one thousand years, Bosnia has existed as a separate province in southern Europe. Located on the Balkan Peninsula, Bosnia was invaded again and again by foreign powers. Over the centuries, waves of migration brought Illyrians, Romans, and Slavs into the region. The Serbs and Croats arrived in the sixth century A.D. By the Middle Ages, Bosnia had grown into an independent kingdom and

annexed (took control of) the neighboring province of Herzegovina.

In 1463 the Ottoman Empire (based in Constantinople, which later became Istanbul, Turkey) conquered Bosnia and introduced the religion of Islam. Many Bosnians accepted Islam during the four hundred years that they were part of the Ottoman Empire. Though Bosnians were all ethnic Slavs and all spoke Serbo-Croatian, the religious traditions and cultural practices of the Ottomans created new ethnicities. The Bosnian Serbs were Orthodox Christians. The Bosnian Croats were Roman Catholics. The Bosniaks in central Bosnia and the major cities became Muslims.

Modern Bosnia is divided into two separately governed states, called entities. The Bosnian Croats and Bosniaks govern the Federation of Bosnia-Herzegovina. The Bosnian Serbs govern the Republic of Srpska. This complex government system was the price Bosnia paid for peace. After nearly four years of fighting, Bosnians were ready to put the war behind them. However, fear and suspicion prevented Bosnians from uniting under one government. In addition, ongoing war crimes trials for those involved in the worst aspects of the war have divided the nation.

Rebuilding their once beautiful country has united Bosnians in some ways. Nearly every road, bridge, city, and village sustained damage during the war. The conflicts that led to civil war, however, have been more difficult to heal. Young Bosnians hope not only to repair the destruction of war but also to build a strong country together.

MARK IT UP

When reading about Bosnia-Herzegovina in other sources, you might notice special marks over some letters. These marks, called diacritics, represent letters in the Cyrillic alphabet (one of the two alphabets commonly used in Bosnia-Herzegovina) that do not exist in the Roman alphabet. For ease of reading, this book does not include diacritics. To learn more about languages and alphabets in Bosnia-Herzegovina, visit the following websites:

BBC Education–Languages: Bosnian
http://www.bbc.co.uk/languages/european_languages/languages/bosnian.shtml
This site describes the Bosnian language and provides sound files of several words and phrases.

Serbian, Croatian, and Bosnian Languages
http://www.omniglot.com/writing/serbo-croat.htm
This site discusses the Serbian, Croatian, and Bosnian languages and shows the alphabets used to write them.

THE LAND

Bosnia-Herzegovina is on the western side of the Balkan Peninsula, which lies between the Adriatic Sea to the west and the Aegean and Black seas to the east, in southern Europe. The country includes two regions that have historic ties that reach back into the Middle Ages. Herzegovina was once an independent province south of Bosnia. In the 1300s, Bosnia annexed Herzegovina to gain access to the Adriatic Sea.

Bosnia is one of the most mountainous regions of the Balkans. Along Bosnia's western border, the Dinaric Alps region divides Bosnia from Croatia and the Adriatic Sea to the west. The Dinaric Alps extend into most of central and southern Bosnia. Successive mountain ranges run from northwest to southeast, making travel across Bosnia difficult.

With 19,741 square miles (51,129 square kilometers) of territory, Bosnia is slightly smaller than the state of West Virginia. Though not strictly landlocked, Bosnia's small coastline of 12 miles (20 km) on the Adriatic Sea has no natural harbor that can receive ships. Other than its small coastline, Bosnia is surrounded by Croatia, which folds

around northwestern Bosnia along the Sava River in the north. Croatia also has territory along the Adriatic coastline on the west of Bosnia. Serbia and Montenegro enclose Bosnia on the east and southeast.

Topography

Bosnia is roughly triangular in shape. With the flat base along the Dinaric Alps in the west, the widest part of Bosnia is the northern and central regions. In the south, Herzegovina gradually tapers toward the Adriatic Sea. Bosnia can be divided into two main geographic regions—the Mountain Region in the north and the Plateau Region in the south.

In the north, the mountains decrease in elevation toward the north and east. Low, fertile plains line the Sava River Basin along the northern border. Most of Bosnia's major crops are produced in the Sava River Basin. The center of the country from the Una River on the west to the Drina River on the east consists of rugged, forested mountains and green valleys. The elevation increases toward the south, reaching altitudes of more than 3,300 feet (1,000 m) in places. Central Bosnia has rich mineral deposits, which people have mined since ancient times. The well-watered land along Bosnia's major rivers has historically attracted settlements in the fertile valleys and grasslands.

To the southeast, more than 70 mountain peaks reach altitudes of 4,900 feet (1,494 m) or higher. One range southwest of Sarajevo is sometimes called the Herzegovinian Himalayas because of its sharp, saw-toothed peaks. Mount Maglic, the highest point in Bosnia at 7,828 feet (2,386 m), rises above the Sutjeska River along the southeastern border with Montenegro.

In the southwest lies a region of plateaus, or flat highlands. One major feature of this region is its karst terrain, where limestone mountain peaks have eroded over time and formed a landscape of rocky plateaus. The dry plateaus support little vegetation. The limestone absorbs the rainwater and forms underground rivers and caves. The rivers run underground until they emerge at lower elevations, or they empty into the Adriatic Sea. Sometimes the caves collapse, forming sinkholes. These sinkholes retain enough soil and nutrients to allow some farming.

KARST TERRAIN

Karst terrain is found in many parts of the world. The word *karst* comes from the Slavic name for "Kras," a limestone region that lies along the Adriatic coast. The word was originally used to describe the dry, barren regions of the Dinaric Alps and the Dalmatian coast in Croatia and Herzegovina. Features of Bosnia's karst region include a large basin near Mostar that is formed from many sinkholes and the Popovo Polje, a fertile valley that measures more than 56 square miles (146 sq. km).

⊙ Major Rivers and Lakes

Dividing Bosnia from Croatia along Bosnia's northern border, the Sava River is perhaps the most important river in the country. The Sava is a tributary of (flows into) the great Danube River, which flows from Germany through southern Europe and into the Black Sea off the coast of Romania. Historically, the Sava divided the Balkans from Europe. Before the civil war, cities along the Sava were the only Bosnian outlets for shipping goods. But the war destroyed most of the bridges between Bosnia and Croatia. War refuse in the river still prevents Bosnia's cities from shipping their goods.

The rest of Bosnia's major rivers flow northward from the mountains.

SLOVENIA

HUNGARY

CROATIA

Sava River

RUSSIA

ATLANTIC
OCEAN

E U R O P E

BOSNIA-
HERZEGOVINA

AFRICA

500 Miles

500 KM

Una River

Sava River

Una River

SAVA RIVER BASIN

Drina River

Sava River

M
O
U
N
T
A
I
N

Vrbas River

Bosna River

R
E
G
I
O
N

*Miljacka
River*

DINARIC ALPS

*Lake
Jablanica*

Neretva

Drina
River

HERZEGOVINIAN HIMALAYAS

*Neretva
River*

*Sutjeska
River*

SERBIA
AND
MONTENEGRO

*Kravice
Waterfalls*

▲ Mt. Maglic

PLATEAU
REGION

Popovo Polje

ALBANIA

Bosnia-
Herzegovina

Feet	Meters	
9843	3000	Mountains
6582	2000	Uplands
3281	1000	
1640	500	Lowlands

Elevation

N

International border
▲ Mountain peak

Adriatic Sea

0   40 Miles

0   40 KM

Following the decrease in elevation, the Una, the Vrbas, the Bosna, and the Drina rivers all empty into the Sava River in the north. The Drina River forms part of the eastern border with Serbia. Melting winter snows in the mountains feed the rivers. As the elevation decreases, the rivers run fast and carve many deep canyons. Rocky terrain also results in many waterfalls along these rivers.

The Neretva River also starts in the southern mountains, flowing northwestward. Near Konjic the Neretva takes a sharp turn and flows southwestward through Herzegovina toward the Adriatic Sea. The mouth of the Neretva River is in Croatia, but Bosnia and Croatia share the wetlands of the lower Neretva. The Neretva River valley is the only natural pass through the Dinaric Alps into Bosnia from the west.

The **Neretva River** winds its way through the mountains of southern Bosnia. For links to websites with more photos of Bosnia-Herzegovina, visit www.vgsbooks.com.

This resort lies on Bosnia's short stretch of coastline on the Adriatic Sea.

Many mountain lakes form in the valleys at higher elevations. These lakes include more than fifteen natural thermal springs, which many Bosnians believe to be a source of healing waters. Fresh mountain spring water is bottled as mineral water. The largest lake in Bosnia is artificial. A dam built on the Neretva River in the 1960s created Lake Jablanica. In addition to the water sports and fishing found around it, the dam serves as a major source of hydroelectric power.

⊙ Climate

Even though Bosnia is close to the Adriatic Sea, the Dinaric Alps along the western border prevent the moderating weather effects of the sea from reaching inland. Most of Bosnia shares a climate similar to that of continental Europe. The overall temperatures are moderate, but winters can be bitterly cold, particularly at higher elevations. In the north, winter temperatures average 32°F (0°C) in January and 72°F (22°C) in July. Average temperatures vary with the area's elevation.

Herzegovina in the south has a warmer climate. Along the coast and the Neretva River valley, temperatures are hotter in the summer and milder in the winter. Mostar in southern Herzegovina averages 42°F (6°C) in January, and 78°F (26°C) in July. Temperatures along the Adriatic coast can reach 100°F (38°C) in the summer.

Snow can be found year-round on the **mountain peaks near Sarajevo.**

In Bosnia snow remains on a few mountains all year, and snowfall is especially heavy on the coastal ranges. The north receives less rain and snow during the winter months, but rainfall in May and June helps with spring planting. The south receives most of its annual rainfall from October to January.

Flora and Fauna

Nearly half of Bosnia's land area is forested. The types of trees and vegetation change with the elevation. Forests of oak and beech are found at lower elevations. Firs and black pines grow high in the mountains. Perucica, one of the last primeval (old-growth) forests in Europe stands near Mount Maglic on the Serbian border. Unlike most European forests, these primeval trees have never been logged. Alpine meadows throughout Bosnia provide grazing for livestock and come alive with

Foxes live in the mountain forests of Bosnia. The quiet habitat of the remote forests is home to many large animals including bears, wolves, and deer.

wildflowers during spring. Hundreds of kinds of wildflowers grow in the meadows. Some grow nowhere else in the world.

In the valleys and in the south, fruit trees flourish. Plums, apples, pears, and cherries grow well in these areas. Plums are made into jam and into a popular brandy called *slivovitz*. In the southern zone, olives, figs, and grapes grow in Herzegovina and along the sunny Adriatic coast.

Many parts of Bosnia's mountains are remote and inaccessible and thus avoided damage during the war. Large areas of undisturbed forest provide good habitat for European brown bears, wild boars, foxes, lynx, and wolves. Deer are plentiful, and in high meadows, wild goats such as chamois thrive. In the lower

PERUCICA PRIMEVAL FOREST

Perucica Primeval Forest is in the rugged wilderness of Sutjeska National Park. Located on Bosnia's eastern border with Montenegro, Sutjeska is Bosnia's oldest national park. Perucica is one of the last primeval forests in Europe. The region is remote, and this old forest has beech and pine trees that are more than 160 feet (48 m) tall. The trees in Perucica have never been logged, and many are three hundred years old.

Neretva River valley is Sutjeska National Park, which preserves a large area of lakes and wetlands for more than three hundred species of birds.

Natural Resources and Environmental Challenges

Although small, Bosnia-Herzegovina has a wealth of natural resources. Mineral deposits of iron ore, coal, bauxite, and salt make mining a major Bosnian industry. Most of these deposits are in the mountains. The nation's heavily forested areas provide lumber and wood products—one of Bosnia's biggest exports. Agriculture isn't a huge industry in Bosnia, but crops include wheat, corn, and potatoes.

Despite its richness in minerals and beauty, Bosnia faces serious environmental problems. The civil war of the 1990s destroyed many areas. Bombs introduced dangerous chemicals into the air and water. Deforestation as a result of too much logging has put some forests at risk. Meanwhile, pollution is also a growing problem. In the cities, cars and factories pollute the air. Farm chemicals and industrial waste get into lakes and rivers, putting fish, wildlife, and people at risk.

One of the greatest dangers to Bosnia's environment is the large number of land mines that were placed along mountain trails and in farm fields during the war. In addition to killing 1,400 people since the end of the war, the mines often kill wildlife.

Cities

The 1984 Winter Olympics took place in Sarajevo, then part of Communist-ruled Yugoslavia. It was the first time the Olympics were held in a Communist country. The games were a great success due to new facilities as well as to the hospitality of the Bosnian people. Bosnia put in a bid to host the 2010 Winter Olympics, but the games were awarded to Vancouver, Canada.

SARAJEVO Before the civil war, Bosnia's population was largely rural. As the fighting spread across the countryside, many people were forced from their villages and farms and took refuge in the large cities. Many people were uprooted by the war, and because census figures are very old, most populations can only be estimated.

Sarajevo (estimated population 387,876), located in a valley surrounded by forested hills in central

Bosnia, is the capital of Bosnia-Herzegovina. The oldest archaeological sites in Bosnia were found at Butmir, a suburb of Sarajevo. Romans came to the valley to enjoy the mountain springs, and a medieval fortified city was located there in the 1300s. When the Ottoman Turks conquered Bosnia, they built the old quarter of Sarajevo in traditional Turkish style. By 1463 the Ottomans had built a mosque (Islamic house of worship), inns for travelers, a Turkish bath, and a bridge across the Miljacka River.

Sarajevo is the largest city in Bosnia-Herzegovina. The Miljacka River runs through the city.

Modern Sarajevo is a blend of Turkish and European architecture. Before the war, Sarajevo was home to Orthodox Christians, Roman Catholics, Jews, and Muslims. The siege of the city during the war destroyed both historic buildings and housing. It killed twelve thousand people and left fifty thousand wounded. After the war ended, Sarajevo's people began rebuilding. The area is rich in natural resources and has a large, educated population. Tourism promises to return when the roads and countryside are cleared of land mines. Sarajevo successfully hosted the 1984 Winter Olympics and hopes to host a future Olympics to help heal the divisions caused by the war.

Visit www.vgsbooks.com for links to websites with more information about Bosnia-Herzegovina's cities—including what there is to see and do, the climate and weather, population statistics, and more.

OTHER CITIES

Banja Luka (estimated population 220,407) is the administrative capital for the Republic of Srpska. Located on the Vrbas River in northern Bosnia, Banja Luka is a major agricultural center. Settled during Rome's occupation, Banja Luka was also a major commercial center under the Ottoman Turks. It continues to be a trading center for the rich agricultural fields along the Sava River. Since the war, Banja Luka has struggled to rebuild its industries. The fertile land and forested mountains provide produce and lumber for Bosnia, but the war interrupted most production.

In northeastern Bosnia, Tuzla (estimated population 118,500) is one of the oldest continuously settled areas in Bosnia. Archaeologists have found settlements older than those at Butmir near Sarajevo. Saltwater springs nearby have been tapped for their salt since ancient times. Tuzla, once the center of industrial production for Bosnia, is also close to the rich mining areas of Srebrenica (estimated population 164,400) and Zenica (estimated population 20,000). Major industries in Tuzla include steel production, mining and ore processing, and power production.

In Herzegovina, Mostar (estimated population 105,448) is the regional capital. The city is divided by the Neretva River and is on the road from Sarajevo to the Adriatic coast. Mostar was the scene of fierce fighting between the Bosniaks and Croats during the civil war. The two ethnic groups have always lived on opposite banks of the river. The war destroyed many historic buildings and bridges that connected the two sides of the city.

Before the war, Mostar had a good economy based on agriculture, textile production, and metalwork. Since the war, Mostar has been slowly rebuilding. A famous Turkish bridge over the Neretva that was built in the 1500s was destroyed in the war. In 2004, with the assistance of international companies, the Stari Most Bridge was rebuilt according to the ancient Turkish plans and connects the two sides of the city once again.

CITY OF SALT

Tuzla is known as "the city of salt" for its rich salt deposits. The Ottomans gave Tuzla its name, which stemmed from the Turkish word *tuz*, which means "salt." For centuries people have mined salt in the area. Recently, the salt was mined so heavily that areas of the city's ground began to collapse, or sink. Some spots dropped as much as 33 feet (10 m).

HISTORY AND GOVERNMENT

Because of its central position on the Balkan Peninsula, Bosnia's earliest history is one of many migrations and invasions. Different peoples entered the Balkans from the north and the east. The earliest inhabitants left behind no written records, but archaeologists have uncovered important historic sites. At the ancient site of Butmir, near modern Sarajevo, archaeologists have found the remains of organized settlements. The stone axes, tools, weapons, and decorated pottery found there date from 2400 to 2000 B.C.

Illyrians and Romans

Sometime around 1000 B.C., the Illyrians moved into the Balkan Peninsula. This group of tribes spoke a language that was somewhat similar to modern Albanian. The Illyrians raised cattle, sheep, and goats. They also sailed the Adriatic Sea, disrupting sea travel by attacking Greek ships. The Greeks of the time wrote that the Illyrians were warlike and barbaric. The Greeks fought many battles against

them, and they respected the strength of the Illyrian soldiers. Alexander the Great, a Macedonian conqueror, took Illyrians with him when he set out to conquer Persia in 334 B.C.

In the third century B.C., the Illyrians were once again attacking merchant (cargo) ships on the Adriatic Sea. This time they were attacking Roman ships. The Romans invaded the Illyrian settlements along the Adriatic coast, and by A.D. 9, they had conquered all the Illyrian land from the Adriatic coast to central Bosnia. The Romans built roads and cities and developed gold and silver mines in Bosnia.

By the end of the third century A.D., the Roman Empire included much of Europe and many of the countries that bordered the Mediterranean Sea. Emperor Diocletian decided that the Roman Empire was too large to be protected and ruled by one man. Diocletian divided the Roman Empire into the Eastern and Western Empires in A.D. 286. The dividing line between the two parts ran through Bosnia.

Emperor Constantine was the first Roman emperor to convert to Christianity.

In 324 the Emperor Constantine moved the capital of the Eastern Roman Empire to Byzantium. The city was renamed Constantinople (modern Istanbul) in honor of the emperor. With the dividing line at the Drina River in Bosnia, much of the western part of Bosnia came under the influence of Rome, the captial of the Roman Empire. The Byzantine Empire ruled the eastern area. In A.D. 395, the division between the Roman Empire to the west and the Byzantine Empire to the east became permanent.

With centuries of history, Bosnia holds a wealth of archaeological finds. Archaeologists have uncovered six-thousand-year-old statues, the remains of ancient cities, jewelry from the Bronze Age, and more. Many of the best finds can be seen at the National Museum of Bosnia-Herzegovina in Sarajevo (http://www.zemaljskimuzej.ba/english/about_us.htm).

◉ The Slavic Migration

By the fifth century, Rome was under attack by tribes from northern Europe. As Rome lost control over its territory, Slavic tribes moved southward into the Balkan Peninsula late in the sixth century. Historians aren't sure where the Slavic peoples originated, but some think they came from northeastern Europe. By the seventh century, the Slavs had settled throughout the Balkans.

The Serbs and the Croatians arrived in the Balkans at about the same time. Some historians believe both tribes came from an area north of the Black Sea, which had a mixture of Slavic and Persian peoples. Both tribes spoke an Indo-European language. Most historians believe that the leaders of these early tribes were Slavic, but others suggest a Persian origin.

The Croats settled west of the Drina River in the area that would become Bosnia and Croatia. The Serbs settled in eastern Bosnia, Serbia, Montenegro, and Herzegovina. The early tribes united under territorial chiefs that ruled over extended families known as clans. For the next five hundred years, a succession of groups that included the Croats and the Serbs ruled Bosnia. The first mention of a separate province of Bosnia came from the records of the Byzantine Empire in 958.

In 1054 the Roman Catholic Church of Rome and the Byzantine Eastern Orthodox Church in Constantinople found they could not settle their religious differences. This resulted in a permanent split in the Christian church. Both churches had sent missionaries into the Balkans, and this division affected many of the people living there. As rulers and kings adopted either the Roman Catholic or Eastern Orthodox faith, the people of their kingdoms also converted.

The Independent Bosnian State

Toward the end of the twelfth century, the first independent state of Bosnia emerged. Ban Kulin ruled Bosnia from 1180 to 1204. Ban was the title used for the early rulers of Bosnia. Ban Kulin focused on relationships and treaties with his neighbors. He encouraged the merchants at Dubrovnik on the Adriatic Sea to develop Bosnian mines. The ruler of Herzegovina

GREAT SCHISM OF 1054

From the time of Jesus Christ's death until the eleventh century A.D., Christianity was a unified religion. Over the centuries, the bishops in Constantinople (Istanbul) and the bishop in Rome began to disagree on matters of language and government of the church. When the Roman bishop told Constantinople that the services must be given in Latin, not Greek, the bishops in Constantinople did not want to obey. The church began to break apart, and eventually the Constantinople branch became the Eastern Orthodox Church. The bishop in Rome became known as the pope of the Roman Catholic Church.

married Ban Kulin's sister. The marriage created friendly relations with Bosnia's southern neighbors.

The land in Bosnia was divided into feudal estates. The noble class owned their land and passed it to their sons rather than to the king as in most feudal systems. This gave the noble class a powerful voice in Bosnian politics. For more than twenty years, Ban Kulin developed the Bosnian economy and managed to keep peace among the landowners.

After Ban Kulin's death in 1204, Bosnia went through a period of instability. To the north, Hungary saw Bosnia as a valuable addition to its empire. The Hungarians were Roman Catholic, as were most Bosnians. Hungary asked the Catholic pope to put Bosnia under Hungarian control, claiming that the Bosnians were practicing heresy (beliefs that go against the church). Ban Kulin had defended the Bosnian church against these charges, but Rome concluded that the Bosnians needed new instruction in Catholicism. Hungary invaded Bosnia in 1238 and occupied much of central Bosnia until 1241. The Hungarian rulers brought Catholic priests to teach Bosnians the accepted way to practice Catholicism.

The Hungarians soon discovered how difficult Bosnia was to govern. The rugged mountains made invasions difficult and slowed the movements of their army. The Bosnians who lived in remote villages rarely cared who controlled the major cities. Even when the Hungarians succeeded in capturing the area around Vrbhosa (modern Sarajevo), the Bosnians kept some territory. In 1241 an invasion of Hungary by the Mongols, a powerful army of nomadic horsemen from Asia, forced the Hungarian army to withdraw from Bosnia. Bosnia lost some northern territory to Serbia and Hungary but kept its independence.

In 1322 Stephen Kotromanic assumed leadership of Bosnia. He sent armies to take back the northern territories from the Serbs and Hungarians. He then conquered parts of Croatia on the west, including a long stretch of the Adriatic coastline between Dubrovnik and Split. In 1326 he annexed the province of Herzegovina. This was the first time that Herzegovina and Bosnia were joined into one country. Kotromanic also worked to improve Bosnia's relationships with its neighbors, especially with Italy and Hungary.

In 1347 Kotromanic asked the Catholic pope to send new priests to teach the Bosnians about Catholicism. He asked that the new priests be able to speak the Slavic language. Kotromanic believed that Bosnia must reform the Bosnian church to establish a good relationship with Rome. The Roman Catholic Church responded by building four monasteries in Bosnia. Meanwhile, Kotromanic converted to Catholicism and, upon his death in 1353, was buried at a monastery.

By the time of Kotromanic's death, Bosnia had developed into a center of wealth and power. But soon the nobles began to fight over who should take over as Bosnia's leader. Many nobles favored Kotromanic's nephew, Stephen Tvrtko, but at fifteen years old, Tvrtko was unable to hold the country together. The fighting forced him out of Bosnia in 1366. He escaped to Hungary but returned to Bosnia a year later to reclaim his leadership.

Tvrtko's power increased as he set out to conquer parts of Serbia, Herzegovina, and Croatia. In 1377 Tvrtko proclaimed himself to be the king of Bosnia and Serbia, though he did not actually rule most of Serbia. By 1391, the year he died, he also claimed kingship over Croatia and Dalmatia. His kingdom included most of the Adriatic coast from Montenegro in the south to Italy in the north. For nearly forty years under King Tvrtko, Bosnia was a powerful force in the central Balkans. But in the east, Serbia was fighting one of the largest armies the area had ever seen. The Ottoman Turks began to move into the Balkans, and by 1392, Serbia fell under the rule of the Ottoman Empire.

Bosnia under the Ottomans

Once again, Bosnia's location put it between two of the world's great powers. To the north was Hungary, which wanted to occupy Bosnia as a way to protect its own territory from the Ottoman invasion. On the east, the Ottoman Turks were building an empire that stretched from Anatolia in modern Turkey to the Balkans. The Ottomans were looking for an opportunity to invade Europe, and the Balkans were a stepping-stone.

In the early 1400s, the Ottomans began supporting Bosnian kings with their military. Meanwhile, Hungary supported a different Bosnian king with their army. By 1440 the Ottomans had captured the mining town of Srebrenica in eastern Bosnia. The Vrhbosna region (Sarajevo) fell to the Ottomans in 1448. In 1463 the Ottomans invaded with a huge army and finally captured and killed the last Bosnian king, Stephen Tomasevic, near Jayce in northern Bosnia. Herzegovina fell around 1483. Hungary recaptured Jayce after the Ottomans withdrew their army, and the city held out against the Ottomans until 1527. After Jayce fell in 1527, the Ottomans controlled all of Bosnia.

The Ottomans governed Bosnia for nearly four hundred years. Other invasions had brought new cultures into Bosnia, but the Ottomans' culture changed Bosnian society the most dramatically. The Ottomans had begun to build the city of Sarajevo at Vrhbosna, replacing the village with new Turkish-style buildings. Sarajevo grew into a major market for traders. The Ottomans, who practiced Islam, built mosques. They also built bridges, schools, roads, and government buildings throughout Bosnia.

The Ottomans also introduced their own style of feudalism to the noble classes. They gave land to Bosnians who were willing to fight with the Ottoman army. Bosnian peasants worked the farms for the landlords. In the early years of Ottoman rule, the peasants were given the right to rent the land in return for a portion of their crops. They also had to pay a tenth of their harvest to the sultan (the Ottoman ruler) in Istanbul.

Religion was the most dramatic difference brought by the Ottomans. The Ottomans were Muslims who followed the Islamic faith. When they conquered Bosnia, most Bosnians were either Orthodox Christians or Roman Catholics. The Ottomans did not force the Bosnians to convert to Islam, but there were advantages if they did. Muslims could own land and carry weapons, and they did not pay the crop tax to the sultan. They did pay a portion of their income to be used for charitable works, but overall, Muslims paid fewer taxes.

In addition, Christian boys could be taken from their parents to be trained in Muslim schools in Istanbul. This system was called *devsirme*, or the boy tribute. The Ottomans forced these children to convert to Islam. Many of them went on to join the sultan's paid army or to serve in the Turkish government. Others returned to Bosnia in government positions. The Ottomans collected many taxes to support

The architecture of these buildings and the Islamic minaret (tower) in Mostar reflect the Ottoman Turk influence in Bosnia-Herzegovina.

their government in Istanbul. They needed their conquered lands' wealth and men to support the empire's wars of expansion. Many Bosnians converted to Islam—particularly in the large cities—in order to participate more fully in city life and the government. By 1625 the majority of Bosnians were Muslims.

The Emergence of Yugoslavia

Under Ottoman rule, government records identified Bosnians by their religion. The Bosnians, therefore, thought of themselves as Muslims, Orthodox Christians, or Roman Catholics. In the mid-1800s, various political movements encouraged Bosnians to identify themselves by an ethnic as well as religious tradition. The Roman Catholics were Croats, while the Orthodox Christians were Serbs. The Bosnian Muslims were seen as Ottomans.

For the most part, Bosnian Muslims owned the land and worked in the Ottoman government. Some Muslims were peasants, but as the ethnic divisions grew, the Christian peasants saw all Muslims as representatives of the Ottoman government.

Throughout the 1800s, foreign powers supported the Christians as a way to take Bosnia back from the Ottomans. Austria-Hungary supported the Catholic Croats in their demands for fairness. Russia supported the Orthodox Serbs whose efforts led to an awakening of nationalism in the Christians. They wanted independence from Ottoman rule in Bosnia. Many Muslims feared that the peasants would demand the right to own land. When the peasants rebelled against taxes, the landowners sometimes used violence to maintain control. The divisions among Bosnia's religious traditions grew.

In 1875 Christian peasants in Herzegovina rebelled against the Ottoman tax collectors. The peasants escaped into the mountains and armed themselves against the Ottoman army. The army burned villages and killed more than five thousand peasants. Thousands more peasants fled into neighboring countries to escape the killing. The rebellions against the Ottomans spread throughout the Balkans. In 1876 Serbia and Montenegro declared war on the Ottomans. The next year, Russia did too. By 1878 Russia had forced the Ottoman Empire to give up much of its land in the Balkans, including Bosnia.

That same year, the Treaty of Berlin ended the war and allowed the Austro-Hungarian army to occupy Bosnia. The foreign powers concluded they needed an occupying army to control the ethnic hatred and constant rebellions that had swept Bosnia. Austria-Hungary assumed the task of occupying Bosnia. The Bosnians fought the Austo-Hungarian army. They wanted independence, not another occupying power. For three months, the Austro-Hungarians fought to subdue all of Bosnia-Herzegovina.

The Austrian occupation continued into the twentieth century. In 1908 the Austrians formally annexed Bosnia. The nationalism that had started in the 1800s fueled the Bosnians' struggle for independence. In

In the streets of Sarajevo in 1878, Bosnians resist the Austro-Hungarian occupation. The Austrians remained in Bosnia until the beginning of World War I.

1914 Archduke Franz Ferdinand, the heir to the Austro-Hungarian throne, traveled to Sarajevo to observe a military exercise. As his convertible car drove through the streets of Sarajevo, members of a Serbian nationalist group known as Union or Death (also called the Black Hand) planted several assassins along the route. The first attempt to kill the archduke failed, but the second was successful. Gavrilo Princip, a seventeen-year-old Bosnian Serb, stepped out of the crowd and shot and killed the archduke and his wife. Princip was arrested and jailed.

In August 1914, when Austria-Hungary discovered Princip's association with the Serb nationalists, it declared war on Serbia. This initial conflict led to World War I (1914–1918). Germany, Bulgaria, and the Ottomans joined Austria-Hungary (collectively known as the Central powers) in the fight against Serbia. Russia, France, Britain, Italy, and the United States joined together to form the Allies and fight on the Serbian side. The larger war had little to do with the Bosnians' desire for independence. But at the end of the war, the Austro-Hungarian Empire dissolved, and Bosnia became part of a kingdom that included Bosnia, Herzegovina, Croatia, Serbia, Montenegro, and Slovenia.

The assassination of **Archduke Franz Ferdinand** of Austria-Hungary *(right)* in 1914 led to World War I.

Serbian King Peter I ruled the new Kingdom of Serbs, Croats, and Slovenes, with its capital city at Belgrade.

When King Peter died in 1921, his son Alexander became king. King Alexander hoped to unite all southern Slavic peoples into a single country. Though the people from the various provinces shared Slavic origins, invasions and occupations over the centuries meant that they spoke several languages and practiced different cultural and religious traditions. King Alexander was unable to hold them together, and in 1929, he created a dictatorship and called the new kingdom Yugoslavia—the land of the South Slavs. The king proclaimed that all the people were unified, but Bosnia and its Muslims had little voice in the politics of the kingdom.

World War II and Tito's Yugoslavia

About twenty years after Yugoslavia had become an independent kingdom, Europe was again on the brink of war. Adolf Hitler and his Nazi Party had come into power in Germany. Hitler and the Nazis had a big following in Germany and Europe, but their ideas troubled many others. Especially troubling were their anti-Semitism (hatred of Jews) and their form of government, called fascism. In 1939 Hitler ordered the invasion of Poland. Britain immediately declared war on Germany, and soon the countries of Europe were lining up against one another. Yugoslavia's prime minister, Milan Stojadinovic, was leading the country because Alexander's son Peter II was too young to take the throne. Stojadinovic built ties with Germany and Hitler.

In 1941 a representative of King Peter II signed an agreement called the Axis Tripartite Pact to support Germany in the war. But the Yugoslavian army, particularly the Serbs, disliked Germany. The army overthrew the Yugoslavian government. Germany immediately bombed Belgrade and invaded Yugoslavia that year. The Germans defeated the Yugoslavian army in less than two weeks. King Peter II fled the country and never regained his throne.

Germany divided the provinces of Yugoslavia and gave them to its allies. Bosnia-Herzegovina were divided between Germany and Italy. The Germans gave power to Ante Pavelic, a Croatian ally, to form an Independent State of Croatia that included most of Bosnia-Herzegovina. Pavelic and his Ustasha Party believed that all the land should belong to the Croats. He also welcomed the opportunity to rid the new state of Croatia of its native Serbs. The Ustasha army forced nearly two million Serbs out of its territory. Their soldiers killed thousands of Serb men, women, and children. At the same

German artillery and infantry enter Yugoslavia in 1942. The German army defeated Yugoslavia in less than two weeks.

time, the Germans and their allies carried out a brutal campaign to destroy Bosnia's Jewish and Roma populations.

The war years were brutal for all of Bosnia's people. In response to the Ustasha killings, the Serbs formed two separate resistance movements. Some Serbs, called Chetniks, wanted a return to a unified country under the Serbian king. Another group of Serbs banded together to fight first the Germans and the Ustasha, then the Chetniks as well. Led by Josip Broz (Tito), this group was called the Yugoslav National Liberation Army (or the Partisans). Tito wanted Yugoslavia to ally with the Soviet Union (Russia) and adopt Communism after the war. Bosnia's Muslims did not identify with either the Serbs or the Croats but died at the hands of both groups.

As the war continued, many Bosnian Croats realized that the Croatian Ustasha was a brutal state. They began to join the resistance movement. Many Muslims joined Tito in hopes of achieving some sort of independence as a separate state. The Muslims knew that if the Chetniks won, they would return to an inferior status with little political voice under a Serbian king. In the course of the war, more than one million people in Yugoslavia were killed, many by other Yugoslavians. The fighting was fierce, everyone suffered, and all sides committed brutalities.

In April 1945, Tito's Partisans captured Sarajevo. Within weeks, all of Bosnia was under Tito's control. World War II was officially over in September 1945, with an Allied victory. In January 1946, Tito proclaimed

Josip Broz, known as **Tito,** was the political leader of Yugoslavia from 1945 until his death in 1980.

a united Federal People's Republic of Yugoslavia. Bosnia-Herzegovina joined Slovenia, Croatia, Serbia, Montenegro, and Macedonia as semi-independent republics under Tito's government. Tito ruled with a heavy hand, and his enemies from the war were killed shortly after he took power. He modeled Yugoslavia's constitution after the Communist government of Joseph Stalin in the Soviet Union. But by 1948, he broke ties with Stalin to retain his country's independence.

Tito followed the Communist system of suppressing religion and putting land and industry into government control. Like all Communist states, Yugoslavia's policy was for the people to put loyalty to the nation above religious and ethnic loyalties. But over time, he created a new and unique form of Communism—one less violently repressive than that of Stalin—that became known as Titoism.

Despite the differences, Tito was still a dictator. He banned both free speech and political opposition groups. But he also gave the Bosnians something they really wanted—peace. For thirty-five years, Bosnians of all religions lived and worked together. As the country rebuilt from the war, Tito often reminded his people that they were all

Yugoslavs. It was not a perfect system, but at least it ensured peace among Bosnia's many ethnic groups.

In 1974 Tito began to plan for the government of Yugoslavia after his death. In a new constitution, Tito gave the six republics and the two provinces of Vojvodina and Kosovo equal power in the federal government. Representatives elected by the republics would each act as president for one-year terms. The president would run the government with a federal assembly. No republic or province would have more power than any other. Each republic and province also had the right to veto any decision made by the federal assembly. The veto power caused some of the problems that led to the breakup of Yugoslavia after Tito's death in 1980.

The Fight for Independence

After Tito died, the unifying force of his personality on Yugoslavia was lost. Once again, the disagreements among the different ethnic groups emerged. The 1980s were difficult times for Yugoslavia. Tito had relied on foreign investment to build the economy. Often the materials needed to operate inefficient industries had to be imported. As the economy declined, people became unhappy with the government in Belgrade. Workers went on strike against the new Communist leaders. By 1990 several republics were planning to secede (declare independence) from the federation.

As it had in the past, nationalism arose among the nation's ethnic groups. Powerful politicians, particularly in Serbia and Croatia, encouraged their people to demand independent governments and territories. Slobodan Milosevic, the president of Serbia, used the military to bring Vojvodina, Montenegro, and Kosovo under Serbian control. With these moves, Milosevic controlled four of the eight votes in the federal government. He rallied the Serbs in the different parts of Yugoslavia. His goal was to unify all of Yugoslavia under a Serbian government.

In 1991 Croatia and Slovenia declared independence. Serbia sent the Yugoslavian army into Slovenia but gave up the fight after ten days and allowed Slovenia to become independent. Next, the Croatian Serbs declared themselves independent from the Croatian government. Serbia sent the army to help the Croatian Serbs fight for a section of Croatia that they called the Republic of Serbian Krajina. Bosnia remained neutral in the war between the Serbs and the Croats, but Bosnians feared that they would face Serb aggression eventually. To escape that possibility, Bosnia's non-Serbs voted for independence in March of 1992. The Bosnian Serbs, led by Radovan Karadzic, declared themselves independent of Bosnia. They formed an independent state that they called the Republic of Srpska.

Bosnia descended into war. The Bosnian Serbs took over any land they claimed as Serb homeland. Groups of Serb soldiers forced Bosniaks and Croats from the villages and countryside in the areas the Serbs wanted. In just one month, more than 275,000 people had to flee their homes. The Serbs also set siege to Sarajevo. For the next four years, Serb mortars placed on the hills around the city continually bombarded Sarajevo. The residents of Sarajevo lived under constant danger of bombing and rifle fire. The bombing destroyed the water and electricity systems. Residents were forced to scour the nearby forests for wood to heat their homes. By the summer of 1992, Bosnian Serb forces controlled almost two-thirds of Bosnia.

At first, the rest of the world seemed unaware of what was happening in Bosnia. To many outside the war zone, it appeared that a civil war had erupted and Bosnians were fighting Bosnians. But soon refugees fleeing the fighting reported that thousands of Bosniaks and Croats were being forced out of their homes at gunpoint by Serbs. Many women were raped, while the men and boys of military age were either shot or placed in prison camps.

The first reports of ethnic cleansing reached reporters and politicians in Europe and the United States at the end of 1992. Ethnic cleansing is a policy in which a majority group (in this case, the Serbs) uses violence and intimidation to rid the land of a minority group (non-Serbs). If the non-Serbs did not leave when threatened, Serbian soldiers killed or imprisoned them. For nearly four years, the United Nations (UN) tried to work with the different sides to settle the war. The UN refused to send

Much of **Sarajevo was destroyed during Bosnia's civil war.** To learn more about the war, visit www.vgsbooks.com for links.

troops, but they sent humanitarian aid for the thousands of refugees both inside and outside of Bosnia.

Finally, the Serbs, Croats, and Bosniaks agreed to meet in Dayton, Ohio, in November 1995 to try to find a way to settle the war. The United States sponsored the talks, which lasted three weeks. In the end, the presidents of Bosnia, Croatia, and Serbia agreed to end the war. They signed the final Dayton Peace Agreement in Paris on December 14, 1995. The agreement divided Bosnia into two separate entities. The Federation of Bosnia-Herzegovina was given 49

> "I keep wanting to explain these stupid politics to myself, because it seems to me that politics caused this war. . . . It looks to me as though these politics mean Serbs, Croats, and Muslims. But they are all people. They are all the same. They all look like people, there's no difference. They all have arms, legs, and heads, they walk and talk, but now there's "something" that wants to make them different."
>
> —Zlata Filipovic, an eleven-year old girl caught in the siege of Sarajevo, in *Zlata's Diary*, November 19, 1992

percent of the land and would be governed by a Bosniak-Croat federation. The Republic of Srpska was given 51 percent of the land and would be governed by the Bosnian Serbs. To make sure the agreement was honored, the North Atlantic Treaty Organization (NATO) sent sixty thousand troops to police the two entities and begin the process of returning refugees to their homes.

The peace agreement helped to settle some of the issues in Bosnia. When NATO sent troops in 1995, they planned to stay until peace was assured. The need for troops continues. In 2005 about seven thousand European Union Force (EUFOR) troops were still in Bosnia. EUFOR is helping with reconstruction, removing land mines, and collecting guns and weapons in all areas of Bosnia. Free elections have been held with foreign oversight, but in recent elections, most Bosnians have continued to vote along ethnic lines. The members of the current rotating presidency are Ivo Miro Jovic

SREBRENICA MASSACRE

In July 1995, between 7,500 and 8,000 Muslim men and boys were killed near the town of Srebrenica. It was the worst genocide (killing a group of people based on their ethnicity) in Europe since World War II. Since the Bosnian civil war, more than fifty mass graves have been found near Srebrenica. Forensic scientists are working with bones, clothing, and DNA (genetic material) to identify the bodies of the victims. Scientists have identified only two thousand of the missing so far. The horror of the massacre helped bring the warring groups to peace talks four months later.

(representing the Croats), Borislav Paravac (representing the Serbs), and Sulejman Tihic (representing the Bosniaks).

◉ War Crimes Trials

The horrors of the Bosnian civil war weren't forgotten after the peace agreement. People in Bosnia and around the world demanded that the leaders who ordered murder and genocide be brought to trial. In the mid- and late-1990s, these war crimes trials were held in The Hague, Netherlands. They were the first European war crimes trials since the end of World War II.

The first trial, which began in 1995, was for a Bosnian Serb named Dusan Tadic. Tadic was accused of carrying out "a widespread or systematic attack against the non-Serb population" during the war. Prosecutors said that Tadic terrorized Croats and Bosniaks in hopes of driving them out of the region. In 1997, Tadic was convicted on eleven counts of war crimes.

More trials followed, including the trial of Slobodan Milosevic, which began in 2002. He was charged with more than sixty war crimes, including "calculated cruelty." With hundreds of witnesses, the trial was still dragging on as 2005 came to a close. Milosevic insists that he is innocent, though most experts agree that he will eventually be convicted.

Other war crimes trials have yet to begin. Radovan Karadzic, the former president of the Serbian Democratic Party of Bosnia-Herzegovina, was charged with genocide for killing as many as 6,000 Bosniaks in Srebrenica. He was also charged with using UN peace-keepers as hostages. But Karadzic, among others, hasn't been caught. Bosnians will have to wait for justice in many of these cases.

◉ Government

The Dayton Peace Agreement approved a two-tiered system of government for Bosnia. The highest level is the central government, which makes national decisions for both Bosnian entities. Every four years, citizens elect three presidents, one representing each of the three major ethnic groups—Bosniak Muslims, Bosnian Croats, and Bosnian Serbs. After the election, the president with the most votes serves as the overall president of Bosnia for eight months. The presidency then rotates to the other presidents every eight months. The president appoints a chairman of the Council of Ministers, who in turn appoints ministers of Foreign Affairs, Defense, Human Rights and Refugees, and others.

The second tier of government is the National House of Representatives, which must approve both the chairman of the Council of Ministers and the ministers themselves. The representatives are elected in general elections. Twenty-eight seats are reserved for the Federation, with fourteen seats set aside for the Republic of Srpska. In addition to the House of Representatives, the government includes a House of Peoples. Local governments select the fifteen members of this body. Five seats are reserved for members from each of the three ethnic groups. The central government makes decisions about foreign affairs, appoints ambassadors, controls the army, and considers all issues that affect both entities.

The two entities also maintain separate local governments. The Federation has a House of Representatives, a House of Peoples, and a president. The Republic of Srpska has a National Assembly, a Council of Peoples, and a president. The entity governments are responsible for local decisions and their education, health, and infrastructure spending.

The Dayton Peace Agreement of 1995 also created the Office of the High Representative for Bosnia (OHR). The High Representative is nominated by the Peace Implementation Council (PIC). The PIC is made up of fifty-five countries and humanitarian agencies that have an interest in a peaceful Bosnia. The OHR works with both Bosnian entities on issues of governance, law, and fair elections. The OHR also advises Bosnians on reforms that are needed before Bosnia can join the European Union. The High Representative will stay in Bosnia until the nation can maintain peace on its own.

Visit www.vgsbooks.com for links to websites with additional information about Bosnia-Herzegovina's history, government, political leaders, and current events.

THE PEOPLE

Bosnia has about 4 million people. The last census was done before the war and put the population at 4.3 million. During the war, at least 220,000 were killed or reported missing. About 1.8 million more were refugees outside the country or displaced within Bosnia. Until a new census is taken, the population total is an estimate. Estimates in 2005 put Bosnia's population at a little more than 4 million.

Most Bosnians—about 60 percent of the population—live in small village clusters and on individual farms. Bosnia is very mountainous, and most farms are small. About 40 percent of Bosnians live in the cities. Bosnia has several large cities that were gaining in population before the war. Large high-rise apartment complexes were built to ease the housing shortages.

◉ Ethnic Groups

Bosnia's ethnic groups have had tense, often violent, relations over the years. The three main ethnic groups are Bosniak Muslims,

Serbs, and Croats. All three groups share some cultural character-istics with groups in the neighboring countries of Croatia and Serbia. The changing boundaries in the Balkan region have often led to war, including the recent civil war. In addition to the main ethnic groups, Bosnia has small Jewish and Roma populations.

Bosniaks make up the largest ethnic group in Bosnia. For many years, they were simply called Muslims to distinguish them from other Bosnians. Recently, the Muslims have adopted the term *Bosniak* to describe their connection to Bosnia. Bosniaks make up about 48 percent of the population. The Bosniaks converted to Islam when Bosnia was occupied by the Ottoman Empire from 1463 until 1878. They tended to live in large cities, especially in Sarajevo, which was built by the Ottomans. Just before the 1990s civil war, large populations of Bosniaks were living in towns along the Drina River in the east, in Banja Luka in the north, and in Mostar in Herzegovina. After the war, many Bosniaks did not return to their homes in areas that became part of the Republic of Srpska. They were afraid to return to the entity that was dominated by Serbs.

The Serbs make up about 37 percent of the population. Most Serbs are Orthodox Christians and share their culture with Serbs living in Serbia and Croatia. Before the civil war, Serbs lived throughout Bosnia. Larger populations of Serbs lived close to the border with Serbia along the north and east. When the war began, the Serbs declared themselves independent of the Bosnian government in Sarajevo. They took control of land that bordered the Drina River and the Sava River on the north and east and land in the southeast near the border with Montenegro.

Because large populations of Serbs had traditionally lived in these areas, the Serbs forced Croats and Bosniaks there from their homes. The Dayton Peace Agreement awarded the Serbs much of this land, which became the Republic of Srpska. In the same way

REFUGEES

The displacement of people from their homes and towns is still a problem for the Bosnian government. By the end of the civil war in 1995, almost two million people were considered refugees. The Dayton Peace Agreement required that the refugees be allowed to return to their homes, no matter which ethnic group they belonged to. Millions of refugees returned to their homes after the war. But they often found people living in their houses or the houses burned to the ground. Even with the success of the programs for return of refugees, nearly half of the original two million refugees may still need help to return.

A Bosnian family sits outside their tent at a UN refugee camp in Zenica.

This is a view of Trebinje in the Republic of Srpska. Srpska has a low population density. The largest towns are found in river valleys. Visit www.vgsbooks.com for links to websites with more information about Srpska.

that Bosniaks were afraid to return to Serb territory after the war, many Serbs left their homes in Bosnian territory and moved to the Republic of Srpska.

Croats, the third-largest ethnic group in Bosnia, make up about 15 percent of the population. The Croats have lived in western and southern Bosnia and especially Herzegovina since they migrated into Bosnia in the sixth century. The Bosnian Croats are Roman Catholics. When the civil war began, the Croats joined the Bosniaks to fight the Serbs. But they also ended up fighting the Bosniaks, particularly in Herzegovina.

Language

The language of Bosnia was once called Serbo-Croatian but now has several names including Bosnian. All of the nation's ethnic groups speak this language, though they call it by several different names. The language is written with two different alphabets: Cyrillic and Latin. Before the civil war, Bosnians learned both alphabets in school, and signs are often written in both alphabets. Since the war, the Republic of Srpska has used the Cyrillic alphabet while Bosnia has used the Latin alphabet.

As with most everything in Bosnia, language has become an important way to determine the ethnicity of the speaker. Although everyone understands Serbo-Croatian no matter who speaks it, small differences in vocabulary distinguish the spoken language in the different regions of Bosnia. For this reason, Serbs speak Serbian, Bosniaks speak Bosnian, and Croats speak Croatian.

The Cyrillic alphabet was named for Saint Cyril, a Greek monk who developed an early alphabet for the Slavic languages in the ninth century. The alphabet was based on the Greek alphabet but includes several additional letters that represent Slavic sounds. Because of Saint Cyril's connection to the church in Constantinople, the Cyrillic alphabet is most often used in countries that practice the Eastern Orthodox faith.

Education

Children begin primary school at the age of seven and are required to go to school for nine years. School is free for all Bosnians. After primary school, children may attend either a vocational or technical school for four years, or they may apply to secondary schools to prepare for university. Secondary school is not required, but many students choose to continue their education. Bosnia has universities at

Schoolchildren follow along in their books as their teacher presents a lesson in a primary school in Sarajevo.

Sarajevo University was founded in the 1940s.

Sarajevo, East Sarajevo, Tuzla, Banja Luka, Mostar, and Bihac. Recently, vocational and technical schools have been popular choices.

The civil war devastated Bosnia's education system. The United Nations estimates that half of Bosnia's schools were either damaged or destroyed during the war. Many schools closed altogether during the war, causing many students to fall behind in their studies. Most of the schools have been repaired or rebuilt since the war. New problems include shortages of trained teachers, lack of supplies, and outdated textbooks. In addition, many areas segregate students according to their ethnic group. The government is working to integrate all public schools, as well as to update textbooks to show a balanced view of Bosnian history.

To learn more about the people of Bosnia-Herzegovina, visit www.vgsbooks.com for links to websites with more information about the nation's citizens.

THE ROMA

The Roma make up a small minority of Bosnia's population. They migrated into Europe from India in the fourteenth century. The Roma suffer discrimination in employment, health care, and education. Nearly 80 percent of Bosnia's Roma children have never been to school. In the early twenty-first century, international organizations set up summer schools for Roma children in Bosnia between the ages of seven and thirteen. For many of them, it was the first time they had ever been in class.

Despite these educational challenges, Bosnia has an adult literacy rate of almost 95 percent. Men often receive more education than women, and their literacy rate is higher, at about 98 percent. Meanwhile, about 91 percent of adult women can read and write.

◉ Health

The civil war in Bosnia dramatically changed the quality of the nation's health care. Before the war, high-quality health care was available to most Bosnians, although access in rural areas was more limited than in the major cities. The war destroyed at least 35 percent of clinics and hospitals, and many of them have not been rebuilt. Many health-care professionals left Bosnia during the war, creating shortages of doctors and nurses. Therefore, Bosnians suffered malnutrition, injuries, and illness with little or no access to health care.

Foreign aid organizations such as the United Nations and the World Bank have dedicated money to rebuilding hospitals and repairing or replacing medical equipment. Even with better access to health care, Bosnia's infant mortality rate of 20 deaths per 1,000 births is much higher than rates in most countries of Western Europe. Life expectancy is estimated at 69 years for men and 76 years for women. Overall, health care and access to it is improving.

Some of the problems that were caused by the war are still affecting Bosnians. Malnutrition was widespread during the war, and many children are still suffering from illnesses such as anemia (a lack of iron in the blood, often caused by a lack of food). During the war, most children did not receive immunizations for childhood diseases such as measles. Since 1992 UNICEF (an arm of the UN) has worked to provide immunizations for major childhood diseases, and nearly 90 percent of Bosnia's children receive needed immunizations.

One of the biggest dangers to Bosnians is the estimated 600,000 land mines that are still found throughout Bosnia. The mines were placed in many areas during the war, and some mined locations are

This billboard warns Bosnians to beware of land mines. Land mines have killed more than three hundred people in Bosnia-Herzegovina since 1996.

still unknown. As a result, mines continue to kill and injure citizens every year. Children are taught in school to stay on the paved roads and sidewalks, to leave unknown objects on the ground, and to recognize signs that warn of mine locations.

Since the war, government officials have worked to eliminate the use of land mines. In 1997 Bosnia-Herzegovina signed the international Mine Ban Treaty, which outlaws the use and production of land mines. Under the treaty, Bosnia agreed to destroy all its land mines in military stock. Also, the treaty helped set 2009 as a goal for clearing the nation of land mines. The goal may be hard to reach, but the effort shows a serious commitment to the issue.

CULTURAL LIFE

Bosnia has a rich tradition of creative expression. Conquering cultures have left behind religious art, architecture, and traditional crafts. Since the civil war, the world has taken an increased interest in Bosnia. For the first time, many translations of Bosnian poetry and literature are being published. The war also inspired photographers and filmmakers to record the lives of Bosnians during the war and to share this inside view with the world.

Religion

About 40 percent of Bosnians are Muslims, called Bosniaks. The Ottomans brought Islam to Bosnia in the 1400s. Muslims believe that the Prophet Muhammad received the words of their holy book, the Quran, from Allah (God) in about A.D. 610 in Arabia. Islam spread quickly as Arab merchants traveled in the Middle East, North Africa, Asia, and Europe. Islam affects every aspect of Muslims' lives. Traditional Muslims follow Islamic traditions

regarding modest clothing, food, marriage, and Islamic law.

The Ottomans converted to Islam sometime before they began to build their huge empire in the fourteenth century. When the Ottomans conquered Bosnia, their empire included many peoples of the Middle East, North Africa, the Balkans, and Hungary. This rich mixture of peoples blended with the Turkish culture and produced great works of art, literature, and architecture in every country in the empire. Since the end of Communist rule in Yugoslavia, Bosniaks have been able to openly practice their religion, which was suppressed under Communism.

Christianity is the religion of both Bosnian Serbs and Bosnian Croats. About 31 percent of Bosnians are Orthodox, while 15 percent are Roman Catholic. When the Christian church divided in A.D. 1054, the Christians in Bosnia were influenced by the missionaries from both the Roman Catholic Church in Rome and the Eastern Orthodox Church in Constantinople (Istanbul). The Serbs accepted the Eastern

Statues of Mary (mother of Jesus) line the shelves of a gift shop in Medjugorje. There are many Catholic visitors to this city, where six children claimed to have seen a vision of Mary in 1981.

Orthodox religion when they were a part of the Byzantine Empire ruled from Constantinople. The Croats, who were closer to Rome, remained Roman Catholic. On most religious beliefs, the two churches are in agreement.

The split arose because the bishops in Constantinople did not believe that a single man, the Roman bishop, should have more power than a council of all bishops. They did not want to give the Roman bishop the power of decision on many important issues. One other major difference is found in the calendar of holidays. The Orthodox Church follows an ancient calendar to calculate the dates of holy days. As a result, many Orthodox holy days are two to three weeks later than the Roman Catholic holidays.

The remaining 14 percent of the people in Bosnia do not belong to any of these three major religions. This figure includes Jews, Protestant Christians, atheists, agnostics, and members of other faiths.

Holidays

Bosnians celebrate a combination of religious holidays and national public holidays. Bosniaks celebrate Islamic holidays that are calculated by the lunar calendar. The exact dates for the holidays and holy months change from year to year according to the phases of the moon. The most important observation is the holy month of Ramadan. Strict Muslims fast (do not eat) from dawn until dusk during this time. In the evening, families gather to break the fast with a special meal.

The last day of the month is called Ramadan Bairam, or the festival of Eid al-Fitr. This holiday is spent preparing special foods and gathering with families and friends. Strings of lights decorate the mosques. About two months after Ramadan Bairam, Bosniaks celebrate Kurban Bairam, or the Feast of the Sacrifice. This holiday celebrates the ancient story of Abraham's willingness to sacrifice his son for Allah. To honor Abraham's sacrifice, many Muslims slaughter a sheep for a feast. They often give extra meat to families that cannot afford to buy a sheep.

The Orthodox and Roman Catholic holidays fall on different days because of their separate calendars. Generally, Orthodox holidays are later than Roman Catholic ones. For example, Catholics celebrate Christmas (the birth of Jesus Christ) on December 25, while Orthodox Christians celebrate it on January 7. In addition to Christmas, Roman Catholics and Orthodox Christians also observe Easter (which celebrates the story of Jesus' resurrection) and New Year's on different days. Before the civil war, many Bosnians joined their neighbors to celebrate the holidays of each religion.

Children light candles at Saint Marko Catholic cemetery during the celebration of All Saints Day (on November 1) in Banja Luka.

National public holidays are Independence Day on March 1, Labor Day on May 1, and National Statehood Day on November 25. Independence Day commemorates the day Bosnia declared independence from Yugoslavia. The Republic of Srpska celebrates the Day of the Republic on January 9 to commemorate the day the Bosnian Serbs separated from Bosnia-Herzegovina.

Food

Bosnian cuisine combines dishes from the many cultures that have lived in Bosnia over the centuries. Many of the dishes are Middle Eastern, Mediterranean, and central European in flavor. Meat is at the center of most meals. Lamb, chicken, beef, and pork are grilled, made into spicy sausages or soup, or roasted. One popular dish is *cevapcici*— grilled sausages served on flat bread. Families serve fresh bread with almost every meal.

Vegetables and fruits are widely available at outdoor markets. Many families shop each day for fresh vegetables, fruit, and bread. Cabbage or grape leaves are often stuffed with a mixture of meat, rice, and chopped vegetables and then baked. Another popular dish is called *burek*. Burek is made by placing meat, cheese, or spinach

A man roasts lamb over an open fire near the city of Jablanica. Lamb is a local specialty.

BOSANSKI LONAC (BOSNIAN POT)

This national dish of Bosnia is easy to make, aside from some chopping.

3 pounds lamb or beef, cut into cubes

1 cup finely chopped onion

1 tablespoon finely chopped garlic

1 cup finely chopped parsley

¼ cup finely chopped celery leaves

1 tablespoon salt

2 teaspoon pepper

3 bay leaves

½ teaspoon hot paprika or cayenne, or to taste

½ cup butter

1 cup sliced carrots

1 cup chopped kohlrabi

½ cup chopped parsley root

½ cup chopped celery root

1 cup green beans, cut into 1-inch pieces

2 red bell peppers, seeded and cut into squares

2 cups tomatoes, peeled, seeded, and quartered

3 cups potatoes, cut into cubes

2 leeks, cleaned and cut into half-inch slices

1 cup coarsely chopped cabbage

6 cups water

¼ cup vinegar

1. Preheat the oven to 350°F.
2. Rinse the meat and pat dry. Combine the onion, garlic, parsley, celery leaves, salt, pepper, bay leaves, and paprika or cayenne. Melt the butter in a large, oven-safe stew pot. Then alternate layers of vegetables and meat, sprinkling some of the onion, garlic, and parsley combination on top of each layer. Combine the water and vinegar and pour it into the pot. Cover the pot with a lid or aluminum foil and bake until everything is tender, about 3 hours. Remove the bay leaves before serving.

Serves 6 to 8

on thin pastry paper. The pastry is rolled around the filling and baked. Families usually eat lunch—the largest meal of the day—together. Soups, stews, grilled meat, and vegetables are common lunch dishes.

Friends and families often gather to have coffee and visit. Cafés are popular meeting places in the cities. Bosnian coffee is thick and strong. Desserts tend to be very sweet, and many are of Ottoman Turkish origin. The most common dessert is baklava, a sweet, layered pastry made with walnuts and sugary syrup. Other favorites are chocolate cakes, apples stuffed with walnuts, and fruit strudels.

Sports and Recreation

Before the civil war, Bosnia's natural beauty drew many people to the mountains to hike and ski. But because of the presence of land mines, hiking and skiing are still not completely safe. Families often stroll together in the evenings and picnic with their friends in the summer. As in other countries of Europe, soccer—which Bosnians call football—is a favorite sport. Children play soccer in parks near their homes. Competitive games are a time for families to cheer on their sons and daughters. The Bosnian national team plays in the European League, while local teams from various cities also compete against one another.

Basketball is almost as popular as soccer. The national team plays in the European League, and many Bosnians also play for other European teams. Competitive amateur leagues for both men and women prepare young adults for play in Europe and in North America. Many Bosnian men and women play for college teams in the United States and Canada. In Bosnia students either play sports or go to the university. The scholarships offered in North America allow them to do both.

The Bosnia-Herzegovina basketball team (in blue) matches up against France in a game at the European Basketball Championships in the early twenty-first century.

◉ Literature

Bosnia has a long tradition of literature and poetry. Some of the earliest writers were religious missionaries who wrote about their work in Bosnia. They used many languages, including Farsi, Arabic, and Turkish, as well as Bosnian. The most famous writer of the twentieth century was Ivo Andric, who won the Nobel Prize for Literature in 1961. He wrote novels about the relationship between the diverse ethnic groups in Yugoslavia. His novel *The Bridge on the Drina* covers 350 years of culture in Visegrad, a town on the Drina River that marks the eastern border between Bosnia and Serbia. Andric also wrote children's stories, essays, and poetry in his long career.

If you'd like to learn more about Bosnian culture, visit www.vgsbooks.com, where you'll find links to sites with information about Bosnia's religions, Bosnian recipes, and further information about Bosnia's literature.

Poetry is popular in Bosnia. Beginning with the Ottoman tradition of poetry written in Farsi, Bosnian poets have written in both literary and popular styles. In modern times, poets have filled a place in the hearts of Bosnians. Mak Dizdar, who died in 1971, is sometimes called Bosnia's best twentieth-century poet. His greatest work, *Stone Sleepers*, is a collection of poems about the unique carved gravestones, called *stecci*, found in Bosnia. Dating from medieval times, the gravestones tell stories about the early Bosnian peoples. Dizdar tried to understand his own history by writing poems about the unknown people buried in the graves.

Architecture

Over the course of two thousand years, many conquerors built cities in Bosnia. The Romans left ruins of public baths, roads, and forts. Roman Catholic missionaries built monasteries in the mountains. The kings of Bosnia built forts and castles. The Austro-Hungarian empire built government office buildings, libraries, and the area's first train stations. This rich diversity of architecture makes Bosnia unique. In large cites such as Sarajevo, Mostar, and Banja Luka, Catholic churches, Islamic mosques, and Orthodox cathedrals stood side by side for hundreds of years.

Architecture reflects the heritage of the people who built it. The Ottomans built mosques, bridges, schools, covered markets, and houses. Some of the finest architects from the Ottoman Empire worked on the bridges and mosques in Bosnia. When the civil war broke out, one of the targets for the different groups was this historic architecture. After destroying the buildings of another ethnic group, the conquerors claimed that the Serbs or the Croats or the Bosniaks never lived in that town or city. An estimated one thousand mosques, three hundred Catholic churches, and thirty-six Orthodox churches were destroyed during the war.

STECCI: BOSNIA'S UNIQUE GRAVESTONES

Stecci are gravestones that are not found anywhere else in the world. Bosnia has more than sixty thousand of these stones. Beginning around A.D. 1200, stone carvers created monuments that began as upraised stones. Later forms were shaped like houses and chests.

Carvers decorated their stones with symbols of their world. Common designs include crosses, suns, stars, moons, and flowers. Some show animals such as deer and horses. Others show hunting scenes, battles, and celebrations. Though archaeologists have studied the stecci for years, no one is sure who began the tradition.

Despite the loss of many buildings, Bosnia still reflects the diversity of its people. With the help of international donations, Bosnians are repairing and rebuilding their architecture. During the war, Bosnian Serbs fired constant mortar rounds into the city of Sarajevo. The mortars destroyed many buildings and started a fire in the National Library. Since the end of the war, the building's exterior walls and the roof have been repaired. But the rare books and manuscripts destroyed in the fire can never be replaced.

Bosnia's National Library in Sarajevo was badly damaged during the civil war but has been rebuilt. To see more images of Bosnian architecture, visit www.vgsbooks.com for links.

STARI MOST BRIDGE

In 1993 Bosnian Croats were fighting their Bosniak neighbors across the Neretva River in Mostar. The mortar fire pounded and finally destroyed the historic Ottoman Stari Most Bridge *(above)*, which had stood since the sixteenth century. After the war, international aid organizations offered to help to rebuild the Stari Most, or Old Bridge. Workers salvaged the limestone blocks from the Neretva. New blocks were cut from the same quarry the Ottomans had used. The new blocks were carved by hand and fit into a plan of the old design. In 2004 the reconstructed bridge opened to foot traffic between the ethnic neighborhoods of Mostar.

In Mostar the Stari Most Bridge, an arched stone bridge over the Neretva River that was built by the Ottomans in 1565, connected the two sides of the city. In fighting between the Bosniaks and the Croats, the bridge finally crumbled and fell into the river. In the summer of 2004, a new bridge made from the same stone and in the same style opened in Mostar.

◉ Visual Arts

Sarajevo has been the home to Bosnian artists for many years. In 1985 Emir Kusturica became the first Bosnian filmmaker to win the Golden Palm, the top award at the Cannes Film Festival (a famous festival in France for independently made films). His movie, titled *When Father Was Away on Business*, shows the politics and family struggles during the first years of Yugoslavia under the Communist government of Tito.

Kusturica also won a Best Director Award at the 1989 Cannes Film Festival for his film *Time of the Gypsies*.

Danis Tanovic, a young filmmaker from Sarajevo, won Bosnia's first Academy Award for Best Foreign Language Film in 2002. His film, *No Man's Land*, tells the story of two young soldiers during the civil war. One soldier is a Bosnian Serb, and the other is a Bosniak. They are trapped in a trench between the enemy lines. They argue over the causes of the war and who is to blame for the destruction of Bosnia. Tanovic uses humor and drama to show the deep misunderstandings that caused the war.

> "What I wanted to show [in *No Man's Land*] was that war is the worst solution—and by doing that, I had the feeling I was making a pro-Bosnian film, because the idea of Bosnia was all different cultures living together."
>
> —Danis Tanovic, Oscar-winning filmmaker, *New York Times* interview, November 4, 2001.

In 1995 a group of young Bosnians held the first Sarajevo Film Festival. Even though mortar fire still battered the city, the festival presented thirty-seven films from fifteen countries. More than fifteen thousand people attended the festival. The Sarajevo Film Festival has become an annual event. It includes a Children's Film Program that brings children from all over Bosnia to view some of the best children's films from around the world. For some children, it is their first opportunity to see a movie.

THE ECONOMY

Bosnia was one of the poorest republics when it was part of Yugoslavia. Because of the rugged terrain, much of Bosnia's land cannot be farmed. Yugoslavia built some major factories to employ Bosnians, but many of the industries and factories were destroyed in the civil war. Almost half of Bosnia's population fled their homes, villages, and farms during the war. Many refugees have not returned. They moved to large cities where they felt safe or went to other countries. Even with the loss and disruption of the population, an estimated 44 percent of the workforce is unemployed.

In addition to the hardships caused by the war, Bosnia is working to build a new economy based on private ownership. Under the Communist government of Yugoslavia, the government owned most industries. Bosnia must find buyers willing to invest in and rebuild the factories. Foreign aid has helped with many projects, but some of the largest plants remain closed. With a changing economy, some of the lost jobs may never return.

The division of Bosnia into two separate entities has slowed economic growth. Each entity traces its own data, but there are no overall national data for production and employment. Cooperation and trade between the two entities is critical to developing an economy that benefits all Bosnians. Tourism is increasingly important to Bosnia, and the relationship between Bosnia and the Republic of Srpska will determine whether tourists choose to travel in Bosnia.

▶ Services

The services sector has been Bosnia's fastest-growing economic sector since the end of the war. It accounts for about 55 percent of the nation's gross domestic product (GDP). The GDP is the amount of goods and services produced by a country in a year. Service jobs are found in areas including education, health, transportation, banking, and tourism. The large number of NATO and EUFOR troops that have patrolled Bosnia to keep the peace contributed to

The **Kravice Waterfalls in the Neretva River valley near Mostar** attract tourists.

the fast growth in services. International aid organizations also contributed greatly to the economy. As foreign aid declines, Bosnia must increase employment without the assistance of humanitarian investment.

Tourism could provide many jobs for the unemployed. Hotels, restaurants, tour operators, and merchants all benefit from an increase in tourism. Bosnia has excellent skiing, hiking, white-water river resources, and natural beauty. Developing the tourism industry could provide many jobs in all parts of the country. The greatest difficulty for Bosnia will be assuring tourists that they have repaired the damage to roads and transportation, have cleared mines, and have cooperated to create an attractive and safe vacation destination.

Mining and Manufacturing

Industry, which includes mining, manufacturing, and related jobs, makes up about 31 percent of Bosnia's GDP. The nation's mountains have large mineral deposits of iron ore, coal, bauxite (for making aluminum), and salt. Since the war, mining output has increased every year. The government hopes that continued growth and processing of minerals will increase exports in the future.

Much of Bosnia's manufacturing is based on processing mineral resources and wood products. Before the war, factories in Bosnia produced cars, trucks, and tractors. Bosnia also produced about 40 percent of Yugoslavia's military arms and equipment. Oil refineries, mostly in the north, produce hundreds of thousands of barrels of oil each day. Since the war, the steel industry has produced metal for rebuilding and for export. The forestry industry produces lumber, wood pulp, and furniture. Wood products are also a major export.

Agriculture and Forestry

In the past, about half of Bosnians worked in agriculture, but in recent years, that number has dropped sharply. Even with a large part of the population farming and raising livestock, the farms were small and inefficient. Most produced enough for their families and some to sell at the local markets. Large crops of wheat, corn, potatoes, and other vegetables are grown primarily in the north and east along the Sava River. Grapes grow in southern Herzegovina.

Grapes grow at a large vineyard in southern Bosnia, near the city of Medjugorje.

Agriculture, livestock products, and forestry make up about 14 percent of the GDP. Sheep are the largest group of livestock, but cattle, pigs, and chicken are also common. Cow and sheep milk are both used to produce a variety of cheeses. Nearly half of Bosnia is forested, so lumber and wood products are important resources. In addition to the large amount of lumber needed to rebuild Bosnia's homes and cities, wood products are a major export. Even though Bosnia has a variety of agricultural products, food products are still a major import.

Energy and Transportation

Even before the war, Bosnia suffered electrical blackouts and shortages of gas and fuel. The power system of thirteen hydroelectric and twelve coal-fueled plants was severely damaged during the war. About 75 percent of oil refineries were destroyed. Immediately after the war, many people were burning wood to heat their homes and cook. Since then the country has imported all forms of energy, though production of electricity has improved. Bosnia produces about 47 percent of its electricity from hydroelectric sources and 53 percent from coal-fueled sources. In 2001 Bosnia produced enough electricity to export. With its wealth of rivers, Bosnia plans to build new plants to produce more electricity.

In the best of times, transportation in Bosnia is difficult. The mountains of central Bosnia require roads and railroads to wind along mountainsides and across deep canyons and swift rivers. Of the 13,570 miles (21,838 km) of road in Bosnia, a little more than half is paved. Of the paved roads, most are only two lanes. Railroad service is limited to routes between the major cities. Flights to and from Bosnia's airports at Banja Luka, Mostar, Sarajevo, and Tuzla are also limited. But the bus system is highly developed, and travelers are able to reach all areas of Bosnia as well as major cities in neighboring Croatia and Serbia.

UNITY IN DIVERSITY

"After so much bloodshed and loss, after so many outrageous acts of inhuman brutality, it will take an extraordinary effort of will for the people of Bosnia to pull themselves from their past and start building a future of peace. But with our leadership and the commitment of our allies, the people of Bosnia can have the chance to decide their future in peace. They have a chance to remind the world that just a few short years ago the mosques and churches of Sarajevo were a shining symbol of multiethnic tolerance, that Bosnia once found unity in its diversity."

—former U.S. president Bill Clinton in a speech given after the signing of the Dayton Peace Agreement, November 27, 1995

The Future

Bosnia made progress toward rebuilding during the late 1990s. With the help of SFOR (Stabilization Force) troops and foreign aid, many damaged buildings, houses, roads, and railroads have been repaired. Bosnians in parts of Sarajevo can feel safe again when they go out to shop or work. They can enjoy the city's many concerts, plays, and films. Most children have returned to school. But even with these improvements, Bosnia has not returned to prewar levels of employment. The economy is coasting, even declining, and nearly 44 percent of Bosnians are unemployed. Many unemployed people feel unhappy and discouraged. If the economy does not pick up and

SFOR: STABILIZATION FORCE

International peacekeepers have been in Bosnia since 1995. The force began with sixty thousand troops at the end of the war. By 2005 those numbers had been reduced to about seven thousand. The SFOR mission is to provide safety and security for all Bosnians so that they can return to their homes. The SFOR also collects guns and ammunition to reduce the potential for violence. Thirty-eight countries, including Europe, Canada, the United States, and South America, have provided soldiers for this important work. In 2005 seven thousand European Union Force soldiers replaced the SFOR soldiers.

Members of the **EUFOR peacekeeping forces** secure illegal weapons in northwestern Bosnia.

Bosnians must leave the country to find work, much of the rebuilding may not matter.

Bosnians fear the ethnic conflict might return if the EUFOR troops leave. The entities are divided in a way that discourages interaction between the different ethnic groups. Separate local entity governments that were approved by the Dayton Peace Agreement have increased the tendency of ethnic groups to live in their own parts of the country. In the most recent national elections, the winning candidates were all fiercely nationalistic. Many experts believe a weak economy and strong nationalistic leaders led to war in the first place.

The Bosnian government is working toward meeting the goals that woud allow Bosnia to join the European Union. These goals require cooperation among all Bosnians. They must agree that the representative national government will have more power than their local governments. The European Union expects them to continue to merge their separate armies into one, both to reduce costs and to prevent future ethnic wars. They must integrate classrooms all over the country and use the same textbooks to teach their children the complex history of their diverse country. They must leave behind the practice of separating children by ethnic group and teaching them a nationalistic history.

Visit www.vgsbooks.com for links to websites with information on Bosnia-Herzegovina's current events, as well as a link to a website with current exchange rates where you can convert U.S. dollars to Bosnian marka.

Separate histories and identities will prevent a unified national identity. Bosnians must work together to build a new country where all have an equal chance at a good life.

Bosnia has already made many changes to create a new unified national identity. The nation has a new flag, a new national anthem, and a single currency issued by a central bank. The entities have the same passports, license plates for their cars, and a shared history that stretches back more than one thousand years. They speak dialects of the same language. A recent survey of young people suggests that the new generation is hopeful and willing to work for better opportunities. Most Bosnians did not participate in the brutality of the last war, and nearly everyone lost someone they knew. When their friends and neighbors needed food, clothing, or wood for their fires, many Bosnians shared their resources freely. Bosnians know how to tolerate and appreciate their diverse neighbors. In the ten years after the bloody civil war, Bosnians are moving toward sharing their land once again. The results of the war crimes trials in the Netherlands will hopefully rule out future ethnic violence. Bosnians must hope that their leaders have learned this lesson for good.

CA. 2400 B.C.   Early settlements of the Butmir civilization are in the area near modern-day Sarajevo.

CA. 1000 B.C.   Illyrian tribes migrate into the Balkan Peninsula.

334 B.C.   Alexander the Great takes Illyrians with him to conquer Persia.

A.D. 9   Rome conquers most of Bosnia.

395   The Roman Empire permanently divides in two, with the Roman branch centered in Rome and the Byzantine Empire centered in Constantinople.

500s–600s   Slavs, Serbs, and Croats migrate into Bosnia from the north and east.

958   For the first time, Bosnian territory is mentioned in Byzantine records.

1054   The Christian church splits into Roman Catholic and Eastern Orthodox branches.

1180   Ban Kulin establishes the first independent Bosnian state.

1204   Ban Kulin dies.

1238   Hungary invades Bosnia.

1241   Hungary withdraws to fight the Mongols. Ban Ninoslav regains Bosnian territory.

1322   Ban Stephen Kotromanic takes over Bosnia.

1326   Kotromanic takes over Herzegovina. For the first time, Herzegovina is part of Bosnia.

1347   Kotromanic asks Rome to send Catholic priests to Bosnia.

1353   Kotromanic dies. His nephew, Stephen Tvrtko succeeds him.

1391   King Tvrtko dies.

1392   Serbia falls under the rule of the Ottoman Empire.

1457   Ottoman Turks build a new city in central Bosnia and name it Sarajevo.

1463   Ottoman Turks conquer most of Bosnia and execute the last Bosnian king.

1483   Ottoman Turks conquer Herzegovina.

1565   The Ottomans build the Stari Most Bridge over the Neretva River in Mostar.

1600s–1700s   Under Ottoman rule, most Bosnians convert to Islam.

1875   Bosnian peasants rebel against taxes.

1878   Austria-Hungary occupies Bosnia.

1908 Austria-Hungary formally annexes Bosnia.

1914 Gavrilo Princip assassinates Archduke Ferdinand in Sarajevo.
      World War I begins.

1918 Bosnia is made part of the Kingdom of Serbs, Croats, and Slovenes.

1929 King Alexander changes the country's name to the Kingdom of Yugoslavia.

1941 Germany invades and occupies Yugoslavia.

1946 Josip Broz (Tito) proclaims the new Federal People's Republic of Yugoslavia.

1948 Tito breaks ties with Soviet leader Joseph Stalin.

1961 Ivo Andric wins the Nobel Prize for Literature.

1974 Tito adopts a new constitution to give equal power to the republics.

1980 Tito dies.

1984 Sarajevo hosts the 1984 Winter Olympics.

1992 Bosnia votes for independence from Yugoslavia. The Bosnian civil war begins.

1993 Mortar fire destroys the Stari Most Bridge in Mostar.

1995 Nearly eight thousand Muslim men and boys are massacred near the town of Srebrenica.
      Presidents of Serbia, Bosnia, and Croatia sign the Dayton Peace Agreement in Dayton,
      Ohio. Bosnia becomes independent of Yugoslavia, but it is divided into two entities: the
      Federation of Bosnia-Herzegovina and the Republic of Srpska. War crimes trials begin in
      The Hague, Netherlands.

1998 Bosnia chooses a new national anthem and flag.

2002 Danis Tanovic's film, *No Man's Land*, wins the Academy Award for Best Foreign Language
      Film.

2005 EUFOR troops replace the SFOR troops that have kept peace in Bosnia for ten years.

COUNTRY NAME Federation of Bosnia-Herzegovina

AREA 19,741 square miles (51,129 sq. km)

MAIN LANDFORMS Dinaric Alps, Herzegovina Himalayas, Mount Maglic, Popovo Polje, Sava River Basin

HIGHEST POINT Mount Maglic, 7,828 feet (2,386 m)

LOWEST POINT Sea level

MAJOR RIVERS Bosna, Drina, Sava, Una, Vrbas, Neretva

ANIMALS deer, European brown bears, foxes, lynx, wild boars, wild goats, wolves

CAPITAL CITY Sarajevo

OTHER MAJOR CITIES Banja Luka, Mostar, Tuzla

OFFICIAL LANGUAGES Bosnian, Croat, Serbian

MONETARY UNIT Convertible Mark. 1 mark = 100 feninga.

BOSNIAN-HERZEGOVINA CURRENCY

In 1998 the Central Bank of Bosnia issued a new national currency called the Convertible Mark (whose value is tied to the euro). The Federation and the Republic of Srpska have the same colors and denominations, but each entity chose its own authors for the front and cultural symbols for the back. The currency is printed in .50, 1, 5, 10, 20, 50, 100, and 200 notes. Coins are issued in 10, 20, and 50 feninga, and 1 and 2 marka.

In 1998 Bosnia chose a new flag. After government representatives repeatedly rejected the designs presented to them by an independent group, the group decided that the design that got the most votes—even if it did not represent a majority—would be used for the new flag.

The new flag was chosen with neutrality in mind. The blue background represents peace. The yellow triangle represents the three main ethnic groups of the nation—Muslim, Serb, and Croat. The stars at the top and bottom of the flag are cut in half so that if the flag was folded, each would form a complete star. This represents the nation's desire to be a single, unified nation.

Bosnia adopted a new national anthem, "Intermeco," in 1998. It was written by Dusan Sestic from Banja Luka in the Republic of Srpska. The anthem does not have any words. It replaced the old national anthem, titled "Jedna i Jedina," which many Bosnian Serbs and Croats disliked.

For a link to a site where you can listen to Bosnia's national anthem, "Intermeco," go to www.vgsbooks.com.

Flag

National Anthem

IVO ANDRIC (1892–1975) Born in Dolac, Bosnia, Andric is the only Bosnian writer to win the Nobel Prize for Literature. He attended universities in Croatia, Austria, and Poland, and his early travels in Europe helped him expand his view of Bosnia. Andric spent three years during World War I in prison for protesting the German occupation of Austria-Hungary. As World War II raged, Andric stayed in Belgrade while it was occupied by Germany. Meanwhile, he wrote three historical novels about Bosnian ethnic relationships. *The Bridge on the Drina* became his best-known novel. In 1961 he won the Nobel Prize for Literature. He donated his prize money to buy books for Bosnia's libraries.

JOSIP BROZ, AKA TITO (1892–1980) Born in Croatia, Broz—known as Tito—fought in both World War I and II. During World War II, he formed a group of fighters that became known as the Partisans. They fought against German occupation and against the Serbs who wanted to bring back the Serbian king. At the end of the war, Tito established a Communist government that united the different southern Slavs into one country. He governed with a modified version of Communism, often called Titoism. His tactics were often controversial, but he was a charming and skilled leader who managed to keep eight different cultures united for thirty-five years.

VESNA BUGARSKI (1930–1992) Born in Sarajevo, Vensa Bugarski was Bosnia-Herzegovina's first female architect. When she went to college in Belgrade in the early 1960s, many people criticized her for trying to break into a male-dominated industry. But that didn't stop Bugarski. She graduated in 1964 and started work immediately. After spending several years working in Denmark, Bugarski returned to Sarajevo. There, she became interested in art and began weaving tapestries. She soon became famous for her ponchos. When the civil war began, she refused to leave, despite the danger. In 1992, as she was walking home from the market, Bugarski was hit and killed by a grenade fired by Serbian soldiers.

ALIJA IZETBEGOVIC (1925–2003) Alija Izetbegovic was the president of Bosnia during the civil war. Born in Bosanski Samac, he was a quiet young man who studied agriculture. He was a devout Muslim, which led him to speak out against Tito's government. He was jailed twice for speaking out against the government. In 1990 Izetbegovic ran for the presidency of Bosnia as a Muslim. He spoke out against the rising nationalism, but he also asked Bosniaks to vote for him because he would protect them. He was elected and served as the president of Bosnia until 2000. Izetbegovic was often criticized for not anticipating the horrors of the war, but when he died, more than 150,000 Bosnians came to his funeral in Sarajevo.

BAN STEPHEN KOTROMANIC (CA. 1300–1353) Ban Stephen Kotromanic ruled Bosnia for thirty-one years. After Kotromanic came to power in 1322, he expanded Bosnia to the north and to the west. He conquered Herzegovina and annexed it to Bosnia. He conquered about 200 miles (322 km) of the Adriatic coastline that had belonged to Croatia. He signed a treaty with Venice and established a good trade relationship across the Adriatic Sea. Kotromanic also invited Rome to send missionaries to teach Bosnians the accepted way to worship. When Kotromanic died, he was buried in a Catholic monastery at Visoko. Bosnia was independent and powerful at the time of his death.

GAVRILO PRINCIP (1894–1918) Gavrilo Princip is sometimes called the man who started World War I. Born in Obljaj, Bosnia, in 1894, Gavrilo Princip grew up under Austro-Hungarian occupation. Princip suffered from a disease called tuberculosis for most of his life. He went to school first in Sarajevo, then in Tuzla. In 1912, when he was fifteen years old, he moved to Belgrade to continue his education. In Serbia, Princip met a group of young nationalists who wanted to fight for Serbia's independence. Princip joined their group and was recruited to assassinate Archduke Franz Ferdinand, the heir to the throne of Austria-Hungary. Princip killed both the Archduke and his wife in 1914. This so angered the King of Austria that he declared war on Serbia. This assassination provided the spark that started World War I. Princip died in prison four years later.

LEJLA RADONCIC (b. 1960) Lejla Radoncic, born in Serbia and Montenegro, founded the Bosnian Handicrafts Project (BHP) in 1995. Living is Sarajevo, Radoncic started a knitting project for Bosnian women in refugee camps during and after the war. The project employed many Bosnian women, including many single mothers who had lost their husbands and homes during the war. After filling a first order for 1,500 sweaters, BHP continued to grow. Radoncic's company employs five hundred women and sells clothing and crafts in stores and catalogs around the world.

DANIS TANOVIC (b. 1969) Danis Tanovic is an award-winning filmmaker. Born in Sarajevo, Tanovic grew up in an artistic family. His mother taught music, while his father worked as a television reporter and editor. Tanovic studied film at the Academy of Dramatic Arts in Sarajevo. After fleeing Sarajevo during the war in 1994, he went to Brussels, Belgium, where he worked odd jobs and went to film school. Tanovic then began to make award-winning documentaries about survivors of the war in Bosnia. In 2001 he made *No Man's Land*, which won the Golden Globe for Best Foreign Language Film in 2001 and the Academy Award for Best Foreign Language Film in 2002.

Before the civil war, Bosnia's natural beauty, friendly people, and cultural diversity attracted many tourists. Since the war, the situation can be risky for visitors. Tourists should check with the U.S. State Department (see the department website at http://travel.state.gov/) for any travel warnings before planning a trip there.

HUTOVO BLATO WETLANDS These wetlands are along the delta of the Neretva River between Bosnia and Croatia. The wetlands protect the nesting and migration grounds for more than 250 species of birds. Other wildlife there includes wild boars, eels, and rare fish.

MEDJUGORJE This town near the western border with Croatia became famous in 1981, when six children claimed to see Mary (the mother of Jesus) on a hill near the town. Since then thousands of people from around the world have flocked to Medjugorje in hopes of seeing Mary.

MOSTAR'S OLD BRIDGE (STARI MOST) The old Ottoman bridge over the Neretva River was repaired according to its original design and reopened to the public in 2004. The top of the arch is more than 65 feet (20 m) above the water.

MOUNT IGMAN SKI CENTER This ski center was built when Sarajevo hosted the 1984 Winter Olympics. Great alpine skiing and beautiful mountain views await visitors.

NEUM This is Bosnia's only city on the Adriatic coast. Coastal mountains and Croatian islands surround the area's scenic beaches.

SARAJEVO Bosnia's capital and largest city offers many sights. The old city is full of history, and visitors can see traditional Turkish crafts and rugs. The National Museum of Bosnia and Herzegovina displays archaeological finds from all over Bosnia. In December the city hosts Sarajevo Winter, a festival in which artists and art lovers from around the world gather. Sarajevo has an active nightlife, with many restaurants, clubs, and plenty of shopping.

SUTJESKA NATIONAL PARK About two hours by car from Sarajevo, Sutjeska is a mountain wilderness. Mount Maglic, the highest peak in Bosnia, is found there. Visitors can also see the Perucica, one of the last primeval, or old-growth, forests in Europe.

ally: a person or country who fights for a common cause

Chetnik: the name for any Serb who supported the return of the Serbian king after World War II

Communism: a political and economic model based on the idea of common, rather than private, property. In a Communist system, the government controls most goods and services.

devsirme: the Ottoman Empire's practice of seizing boys and forcing them to convert to the religion of Islam

dictator: a leader who completely controls a country, often repressing rights such as free speech

entity: an independent, self-governing region

Islam: a religion founded on the Arabian Peninsula in the seventh century A.D. by the Prophet Muhammad. The religion's primary tenets are known as the Five Pillars of Islam. Most followers of Islam, including most Bosniaks, called Muslims, are members of the Sunni sect, while others follow the Shiite branch of the religion.

mosque: an Islamic place of worship

nationalism: a philosophy that emphasizes loyalty to one's own nation above all else. Nationalist goals may include preservation of national culture, fulfillment of the nation's needs, and the nation's independence from outside influence.

Orthodox Christianity: also called Eastern Orthodoxy, this religion is a branch of Christianity that broke off from the Roman Catholic Church in 1054. Many residents of Serbia and Montenegro follow Eastern Orthodox Christianity.

peasant: a farmer of a low-ranking social class

privatization: the transfer of ownership of businesses, goods, and other assets from government (public) to individual (private) control

refugee: a person who has been forced to flee his or her home country to escape danger

Roman Catholic Christianity: a branch of Christianity that followed the pope in Rome after the Christian church broke up in the eleventh century A.D.

secede: to formally declare independence from a country

Slavs: members of an ethnic group, sometimes called a tribe, that was believed to originate in eastern Europe. Slavs share a language family as well as a historical background.

Titoism: the kind of Communism employed by Josip Broz (Tito), Yugoslavia's leader from 1945 to 1980. Titoism did not follow the style and pattern of Soviet Communism and was generally less restrictive.

Selected Bibliography

Clissold, Stephen. ed. *A Short History of Yugoslavia: From Early Times to 1966.* **Cambridge, UK: Cambridge University Press, 1966.**
This survey offers useful information on Bosnia-Herzegovina's history as part of Yugoslavia, ending about midway through Tito's time in power.

CNN.com. **2005.**
http://www.cnn.com **(December 1, 2005).**
This site provides current events and breaking news about Bosnia-Herzegovina, as well as a searchable archive of older articles.

Europa World Yearbook. Vol. 1. London: Europa Publications Ltd., 2003.
This reference book contains information on Bosnia and each of the world's nations, including statistics, essays, and descriptions of government and economics.

Glenny, Misha. *The Balkans: Nationalism, War and the Great Powers: 1804–1999.* **New York: Penguin Books, 2001.**
Former central European correspondent for the BBC, Glenny goes back two hundred years and illustrates how the Yugoslavian civil war might have been expected. A glossary and extensive bibliography are included.

————*The Fall of Yugoslavia: The Third Balkan War.* **New York: Penguin Books, 1992.**
A former BBC correspondent, Glenny writes with firsthand knowledge and passion about the breakup of Yugoslavia. The book follows the conflict and its leaders from 1990 to 1992.

Lovrenovic, Ivan. *Bosnia: A Cultural History.* **New York: New York University Press, 2001.**
Bosnian author Lovrenovic covers Bosnia from Paleolithic times to the present from a cultural perspective. The book includes a discussion of art, music, and architecture through the ages, as well as a glossary, timeline, bibliography, and historical maps.

Maass, Peter. *Love Thy Neighbor: A Story of War.* **New York: Knopf, 1996.**
This compelling, firsthand account of what Bosnians thought in the midst of war. Maass, a staff writer for the *Washington Post*, makes readers question their own biases as well.

Malcolm, Noel. *Bosnia: A Short History.* **New York: New York University Press, 1994.**
Malcolm offers an excellent overview of the history of Bosnia. The book covers earliest migrations and includes a thoughtful analysis of the destruction of Yugoslavia.

Mazower, Mark. *The Balkans: A Short History.* **New York: Random House, 2000.**
Written by a professor of history, this source describes the land, conquests, and culture of the Balkan Peninsula and includes a timeline, maps, and a bibliography.

Pinson, Mark., ed. *The Muslims of Bosnia-Herzegovina.* Cambridge, MA: Harvard University Press, 1996.
This collection of essays by Balkan experts covers the history of Bosnian Muslims from medieval times until 1992 and provides detailed print and electronic sources.

ReliefWeb: Countries and Emergencies: Bosnia and Herzegovina. 2005.
http://www.reliefweb.int/rw/dbc.nsf/doc104?OpenForm&rc=4&cc=bih
(December 1, 2005).
This site presents information on humanitarian concerns in Bosnia and Herzegovina, including food supply, land mines, and more.

Turner, Barry, ed. *The Statesman's Yearbook: The Politics, Cultures, and Economies of the World,* 2003. New York: Macmillan Press, 2003.
This resource provides concise information on Bosnia-Herzegovina's history, climate, government, economy, and culture, including relevant statistics.

Further Reading and Websites

Agee, Chris, ed. *Scar on the Stone: Contemporary Poetry from Bosnia.* **Newcastle upon Tyne, UK: Bloodaxe Books Ltd., 1998.**
This is a collection of works by twenty-five contemporary Bosnian poets in English translation, most of whom are unknown outside of Bosnia. Poems are followed by essays that illustrate Bosnian life. Most translators are poets themselves.

"Background Note: Bosnia and Herzegovina." *U.S. Department of State.*
http://www.state.gov/r/pa/ei/bgn/2868.htm
The U.S. Department of State's Web page on Bosnia-Herzegovina includes facts and figures about the nation's people, geography, economy, and more.

Black, Eric. *Bosnia: Fractured Region.* **Minneapolis: Lerner Publications Company, 1999.**
Black offers an excellent overview of the events that led to the war in Bosnia.

Bosnia Institute.
http://www.bosnia.org.uk
This institute provides current information on Bosnia. News articles, an interactive map, and a newsletter are included.

Bran, Zoe. *After Yugoslavia.* **Oakland, CA: Lonely Planet Publications, 2001.**
In 1999 Scottish travel writer Zoe Bran returned to the newly independent countries of the former Yugoslavia to see what had changed. She originally traveled to Yugoslavia as a tourist in 1978. Bran describes the changes to the landscape, cities, and people caused by the wars. She tries to understand the reasons for the violence that tore Yugoslavia apart.

Clancy, Tim. *Bosnia and Herzegovina: The Bradt Travel Guide.* **Guilford, CT: Globe Pequot Press Inc., 2004.**
This is the first updated Bosnian travel guide in English since the war. Clancy has lived in Bosnia since1992 and works as a consultant to Bosnia's tourism office.

Filipovic, Zlata. *Zlata's Diary: A Child's Life in Sarajevo.* **New York: Penguin Books, 1995.**
Zlata Filipovic began her diary at the age of eleven and soon realized that Bosnia was at war. For two years, Zlata recorded what she saw and how she felt during the siege of Sarajevo.

Fratkin, Leslie. *Sarajevo Self-Portrait: The View from Inside.* **New York: Umbrage Books, 2000.**
A beautiful collection of photographs from nine Bosnian photographers taken in Sarajevo during the war. Photos are accompanied by essays written by the photographers.

Green Visions: Bosnia and Herzegovina
http://www.greenvisions.ba/gv/clanak.php?lang=2&kat=5
This site provides information on the ecology and parks of Bosnia. It provides good photographs and descriptions of ecology tours are offered each year.

Marcovitz, Hal. *The Balkans: People in Conflict*. **Philadelphia: Chelsea House, 2002.**
This book examines the troubled recent history of the Balkan Peninsula.

The New York Times on the Web.
http://www.nytimes.com
This online version of the newspaper offers current news stories along with an archive of articles on Bosnia-Herzegovina.

Schiffman, Ruth. *Josip Broz Tito*. **New York: Chelsea House, 1987.**
This biography explores the life and political career of Tito.

Silverman, Robin Landew. *A Bosnian Family*. **Minneapolis: Lerner Publications Company, 1997.**
A close look at the war and its effect on one family. The book follows them as they escape from their city in Bosnia, through a refugee camp and, finally, to a new life in North Dakota.

Tekavec, Valerie. *Teenage Refugees from Bosnia-Herzegovina Speak Out*. **New York: Rosen Publishing Group, 1995.**
Eight teenagers from different ethnic groups and parts of Bosnia describe leaving their homes to escape the war and finding themselves in a new culture.

vgsbooks.com
http://www.vgsbooks.com
Visit vgsbooks.com, the home page of the Visual Geography Series®. You can get linked to all sorts of useful online information, including geographical, historical, demographic, cultural, and economic websites. The vgsbooks.com site is a great resource for late-breaking news and statistics.

World Factbook 2005: Bosnia and Herzegovina.
http://cia.gov/cia/publications/factbook/geos/bk.html
The entry for Bosnia-Herzegovina in the CIA's *World Factbook* includes detailed statistics about the nation.

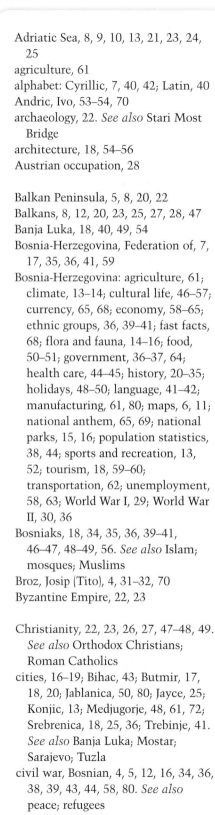

Captions for photos appearing on cover and chapter openers:

Cover: This bridge in the town of Mostar was built in 1566. It was destroyed in the Bosnian civil war in the 1990s but was rebuilt afterward.

pp. 4–5 A view of Bosnia-Herzegovina from Croatia to the north

pp. 8–9 The Dinaric Alps rise above the Neretva River valley near Jablanica in southern Bosnia-Herzegovina.

pp. 38–39 A street scene in Sarajevo, the nation's capital

pp. 46–47 Muslim men pray in front of a Sarajevo mosque on the festival day of Eid al-Fitr.

pp. 58–59 A worker measures the temperature of steel at a steel mill in Zenica. Metal production is important for rebuilding in Bosnia-Herzegovina.

Photo Acknowledgments

Images in this book are used with permission of: © Martin Barlow/Art Directors, pp. 4–5, 8–9, 12, 43, 48 (top), 50, 55, 61; © XNR Productions, pp. 6, 11; © Mario Corvetto/Evergreen Photo Alliance, p. 14; PhotoDisc Royalty Free by Getty Images, p. 15; NATO PHOTO, p. 17; © Time Life Pictures/Mansell/Time Life Pictures/Getty Images, p. 22; © David Bell/Art Directors, p. 26; © Mary Evans Picture Library, p. 28; Library of Congress (LC-DIG-ggbain-07650), p. 29; © Keystone/Getty Images, pp. 31, 32; © Howard Sayer/Art Directors, pp. 34–35, 40; © J.Kaman/Travel-Images.com, pp. 38–39, 45, 60; © M.Torres/Travel-Images.com, p. 41; © Ibrahim/Art Directors, p. 42; © Reuters/CORBIS, pp. 46–47; © STRINGER/AFP/Getty Images, pp. 48–49, 63; © JESSICA GOW/AFP/Getty Images, p. 52; © KPA/ZUMA Press, p. 53; © Malcolm Jenkin/Art Directors, p. 56; © Danilo Krstanovic/Reuters/CORBIS, pp. 58–59; Audrius Tomonis–www.banknotes.com, p. 68.

Cover: © Michael S. Yamashita/CORBIS. Back cover photo: NASA.